Edisto Beach: A Bottle Tree Scavenger Hunt

Carolyn Rizer Kight

Dedication

To my real-life Sweetgrass Kids - Island Ella, Saltwater Ben, Sassafras Ro, Cattail Cal, Heavenly Haven, Grouper Grady, and those Kids yet to come - this is for you! You inspire every Mimi tale and every adventure set in the Edisto backdrop. I love each of you the purplest and for every unique quality you possess. However, I think indulging me all these years with our nightly crab stories and daily scavenger hunts are among the most special of memories! Here's to always carrying around baby sharks and cookies!

-Mimi

To all of my lifelong friends that roamed the waterways of Edisto with me (you know who you are!), our memories are beyond treasured and a big part of why this place is so special.

Bottle Tree Folklore

Traveling through America's history-filled, moss-draped, old southern coastal regions you may come upon a truly intriguing tradition kept alive by island people and our local Gullah residents. It is a centuries-old storyline involving something called a "bottle tree". The trees are visible in many Lowcountry yards where salt air gently blows and pluff mud smells of a recognizable scent more alluring to some than the most expensive perfume. These fascinating structures are thought to date back to origins in West African, Egyptian, and Mesopotamian cultures. Bottle trees are not exactly living trees as we know them, but are historically important to many people.

The bottle tree folklore found its way to America in the 1600s. People new to the area, especially ones from the Congo region of Africa, often placed bottles on whatever dead tree branches were available yet seemed to prefer the branches of myrtle trees. These trees held biblical significance in several mentions. One of these mentions includes Zechariah's vision where he stood "among the myrtle trees". These trees reportedly symbolized youth, peace, love and prosperity. If the locals had access to the right materials, they also may have placed them on rods formed into tree shapes. These so-called iron tree shapes have been fabricated in the American Southeast for hundreds of years.

Bottle trees and the accompanying stories passed down through the generations are truly fascinating. According to the tradition, colorful bottles hung upside down near important locations such as homes, road intersections, churches, or local gathering spots with the intention of trapping infestations of evil spirits. The legend stated that the traditional rich cobalt blue color of the bottles had the power to heal all types of ailments. It was this healing power that enticed the spirits to enter the bottles. Once they entered, they would be imprisoned and unable to get out. The following morning, when the hot southern sun rose from the watery horizon, the trapped evil spirits would vanish within the bottles and the area would be cleansed of their mischievous wrongdoings. Obviously, they did not fair well within their humid cobalt blue environments during the heat of the day! The story also claimed if a bottle hummed when the wind blew through its branches, a spirit remained trapped alive deep inside the glass. You may want to listen for any humming sounds as you proceed from this point forward... just in case!

Today, bottle trees and other bottle decorations are sometimes called "poor man's stained glass". Beautiful jewel tones of cobalt blue, forest green, citrine yellow, ruby red and a variety of other wonderful colors can still be seen across the South today... especially at Edisto! The displays are now mostly decorative and just plain fun. Edisto Beach adorns such a variety of trees that finding them is a real treat!

Please enjoy getting to know our unique barrier island and its highly unique and respected culture as you begin your scavenger hunt adventure. Try the course yourself or add in a family challenge with golf carts and bikes allowing for some fun-friendly competition! Time yourself from the word "GO" to discover all 16 trees. Back at your house or campsite, you can share all of the hilarious island stories that make an Edisto adventure always one of a kind! I hope you enjoy our beloved island but let me caution you to be respectful of private property and view the trees from a distance. Stay on public roads and no touching trees, please! We want all of our residents to happily continue providing trees for our Edisto scavenger hunts.

Rules:

There are 16 bottle trees. Each tree has a picture of the tree and anywhere from 1 to 4 hints of its location. The hint may or may not give away its "exact' location so look around, walk up the street a bit. It will be close by. As you find each tree, check that one off on the line provided. When you have found all 16, rush back to your designated spot and take a picture of yourself or your group holding up this book. Post this picture and your time on the Edisto Bottle Tree Scavenger Hunt FB page so you can compare your group's time to other groups!

Winnings you ask?... a very special fun day with fun people discovering our most treasured SC Lowcountry barrier island!

Note your time here:

_____ TREE #1

HINT 1
At Murray and Myrtle stands our first
tree to be found.
The cobalt leaves are all filled and not
one on the ground.

HINT 2
Should you have a question or emergency
for the town,
turn by this tree and to those services
you're bound

_____ TREE #2

HINT 1
This small road is off the well-beaten path,
yet, close to playing Bingo you do
the math

HINT 2
This "cap" is not for your salty ol' head,
but a wave in the ocean a calm day
should dread

_____ TREE #3

HINT 1
*These Clemson fans may be proud
of this orange paw...
but the garnet and black say, "We
have the colors of SC, ya'll!"*

HINT 2
*The whitetails graze around this
tree all a sport,
'cause the area is quiet near "Edisto"
and "Fort"*

_____ TREE #4

HINT 1
Closer to "Edisto" than the Tiger Paw tree lies green and blue bottles, look closely and you'll see

HINT 2
Up on a hill grows a bottle treasure trove, right there on "Fort" by an ol' cookstove.

____TREE #5

HINT 1
If you drive down this back beach street,
the #5 tree will be a nice treat.

HINT 2
The house is so happy, a yellow of sorts,
along the same back road that rhymes with "Port"

____TREE # 6

HINT 1
This bottle tree is quite a piece of art.
The ladder climb alone was way off the chart!

HINT 2
Have you ever noticed this corner of Lybrand?
Four stop signs or more, so look closely if you can!

_____ TREE # 7

HINT 1
This tree hangs like a bunch of bananas...
or an upside-down mountain from the state of Montana

HINT 2
There's a pair of birds that would rather not be single
They love their friends and love to FLEMMINGLE!

We're close to the end of "JUNGLE" that we talked about before
You may see a lot of stop signs, three maybe four!

_____ TREE #8

HINT 1
This spirit catcher is on one of two major roads.
*Look very closely, it fails to be **bold**.*

HINT 2
The colors are varied, not all cobalt blue.
The greens stand out and the browns do, too.

_____ TREE #9

It's at the end of the "ATLANTIC" and in great camouflage.
The mostly green leaves cling close to a fence and can look like a mirage.

____TREE #10

HINT 1
Back on this quaint little road, spanish moss hangs low.
It's fingers will lull you as it waves to and fro.

HINT 2
The "ATLANTIC" lies at one end, the "JUNGLE" near the other...
A "DOLPHIN" swims where this tree stands - a long way from its mother.

____ TREE #11

HINT 1
Bottle trees like to play at parks with
tigers and "LYONS".
For if at first, you cannot find, I suggest
you keep on tryin'.

HINT 2
A walk on PORTIA to this tree - whether from
PALMETTO or JUNGLE ROAD-
will leave you about equal distance from either
I am told.

____ TREE #12

This tree with high branches lives near someone named "MARY".
Seagulls love to fly here but never to tarry.

HINT 2
Golf carts, house rentals, and cows are found close by.
The cows appear quite hungry, while the carts offer a try.

____TREE #13

HINT 1
This tree is near a "planet" on the front boulevard.
You can walk to eat seafood or pizza for neither is far.

HINT 2
"FINS" live behind this glistening glass sapling.
The spirits they caught have hopefully stopped thrashing!

HINT 3
Not too far from Whaley's is a cobalt blue tree,
where feathery branches grow for all of us to see.

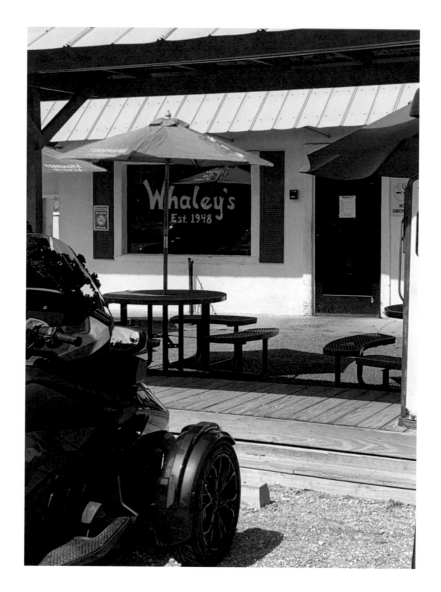

____TREE #14

This curvy eye catcher is a sign of folklore and hospitality.
It's located close to our friends at Edisto Realty.

The colors on this tree are all so very fun!
Watch out for your spirits, they really catch the sun.

____TREE #15

HINT 1
*The road shares a name with a bridge
and a river,
but spirits hiding here may want to
reconsider.*

HINT 2
*Some evil spirits may THINK they're hidden
behind this ol' live oak,
but they should know that this hunt is
CERTAINLY NO JOKE!*

HINT 3
It's cobalt blue leaves are absolutely looking
rather snappy,
while it's message suggests "No worries...JUST
BE HAPPY!"

HINT 4
The green tree topper stands out with beauty
and looks something like a heart.
The owner who put this tree together created a
work of art!

____TREE #16

HINT 1
*These spirits are the only ones you have to drive
and see. It requires a sharp right turn beside the
Mystery Tree!*

HINT 2
*The way is quite gorgeous, under secret
canopies you'll go.
Better watch out for the bumps, they will toss to
and fro!*

HINT 3
Your last tree will be close to where history lies in wait.
Look for the spinning daisies by a white wooden gate.

You are finished, now scoot! You aren't too far!
Back to the beach in your trusty ol' car!

Hope you enjoyed our scavenger hunt and that you enjoy the rest of your visit to Edisto!

Disclaimer: With storms and constant real estate movement there exists the possibility that some bottle trees on this hunt may not always be on the course for us to enjoy. Situations change on Edisto constantly as it does everywhere. Should this become the case, please understand and enjoy those remaining trees we are so very fortunate to have on the island.

Made in the USA
Columbia, SC
29 November 2024